Lett

MW00720297

SCHOOL PUBLISHERS

Photos:
Cover, © Shutterstock; p. 2, © Shutterstock; p. 3, © Harcourt Telescope; p. 4, © Superstock;
p. 5, © Superstock; p. 6, © Harcourt Telescope; p. 7, © Harcourt Telescope; p. 8, © Superstock.

Printed in China

ISBN 10: 0-15-358385-1
ISBN 13: 978-0-15-358385-8

Ordering Options
ISBN 10: 0-15-358355-X (Grade K Below-Level Collection)
ISBN 13: 978-0-15-358355-1 (Grade K Below-Level Collection)
ISBN 10: 0-15-360638-X (package of 5)
ISBN 13: 978-0-15-360638-0 (package of 5)

4 5 6 7 8 9 10 0940 15 14 13 12 11 10 09

q

q

q

q

q

q

q